Phonics Skills

Level 1

Teacher's Annotated Edition

A Division of The McGraw-Hill Companies

Columbus, Ohio

www.sra4kids.com

SRA/McGraw-Hill

*A Division of The **McGraw·Hill** Companies*

Send all inquiries to:
SRA/McGraw-Hill
8787 Orion Place
Columbus, OH 43240-4027

Printed in the United States of America.

ISBN 0-07-570200-2

4 5 6 7 POH 07 06 05 04

Table of Contents

Writing Letters

A A A A A A A A A

a a a a a a a a a

B B B B B B B B

b b b b b b b b b

▶ Writing Letters

C C C C C C C C

c c c c c c c c c c

D D D D D D D D D

d d d d d d d d d d

Name ______________________ Date __________

Writing Letters

Directions: Write as many letters as will fit on each line of these practice pages.

E E E E E E E

e e e e e e e e e e

F F F F F F F

f f f f f f f f f f f f f

G G G G G G G

g g g g g g g g g

▶ Writing Letters

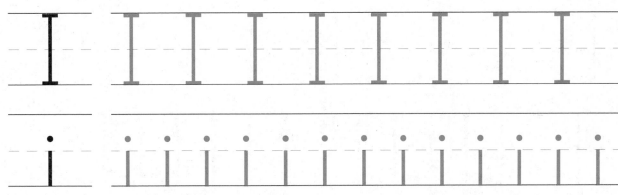

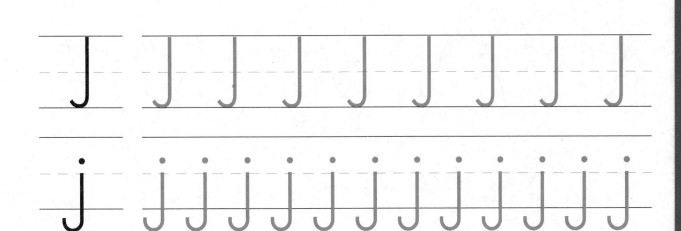

▶ Writing Letters

Directions: Write as many letters as will fit on each line of these practice pages.

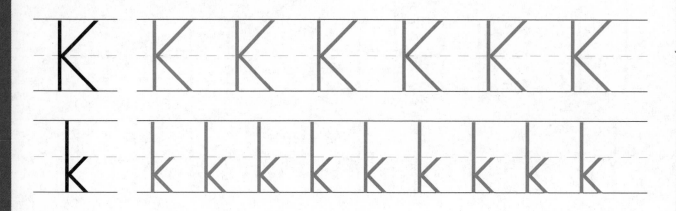

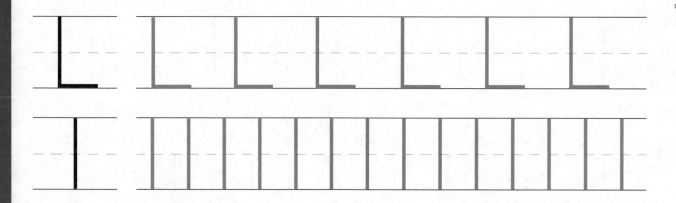

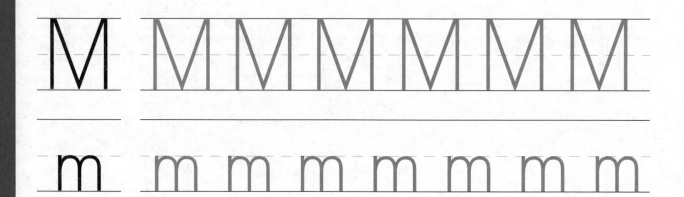

Writing Letters

Directions: Write as many letters as will fit on each line of these practice pages.

N N N N N N N N N N

n n n n n n n n n n

O O O O O O O O

o o o o o o o o o o

P P P P P P P P

p p p p p p p p p p

▶ **Writing Letters**

Q   Q Q Q Q Q Q

q   q q q q q q q q

R   R R R R R R

r   r r r r r r r r r r

S   S S S S S S

s   s s s s s s s s s s

▶ Writing Letters

Directions: Write as many letters as will fit on each line of these practice pages.

T T T T T T T

t t t t t t t t t t t t t t t

U U U U U U U

u u u u u u u u u u

V V V V V V V

v v v v v v v v v v v v

▶ **Writing Letters**

Directions: Write as many letters as will fit on each line of these practice pages.

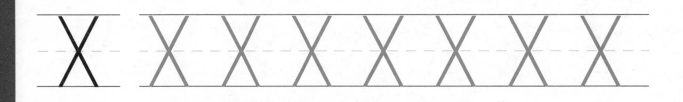

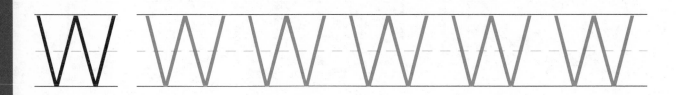

Letter Knowledge • **Phonics Skills**

▶ Writing Letters

Directions: Write as many letters as will fit on each line of these practice pages.

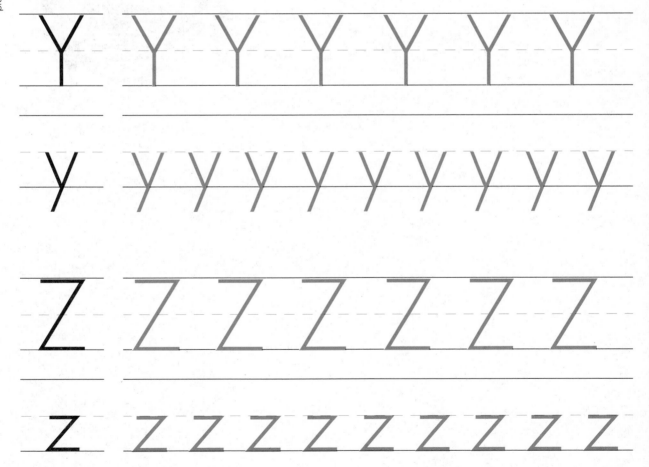

UNIT 1   Let's Read! • **Lesson 10** *Twinkle Twinkle Firefly*

Capital and Lowercase Letters

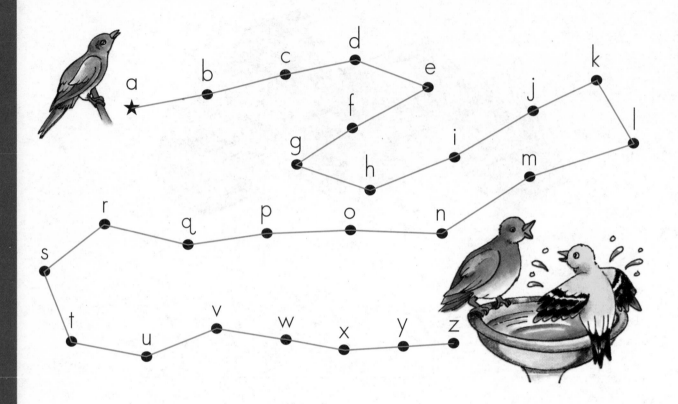

Letter Knowledge • Phonics Skills

▶ **Capital and Lowercase Letters**

Directions: Connect the dots from A to Z.

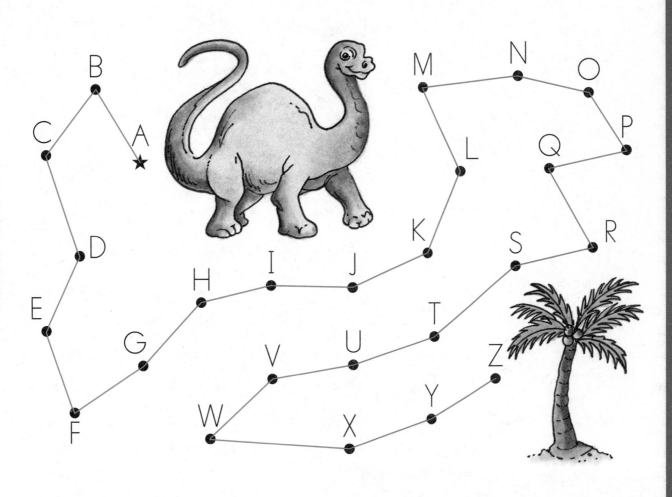

▶ Sounds and Spellings

Directions: Practice writing s and S, then write s under each picture whose name begins with /s/.

S

s s s s s s s s s s s

S S S S S S

▶ Listening for Consonants

___ S ___   ___ S ___   ___ S ___

▶ **Listening for Consonants**

Directions: Write s next to each picture that begins with /s/.

 _____ S

_____ S

 _____ S

 _____ S

 _____
_____

 _____
_____

 _____ S

_____ S

Sounds and Spellings

Directions: Practice writing *m* and *M*. Then write *m* under each picture that has an /m/ sound in it.

m

m m m m m m m

M M M M M M M M

Listening for Consonants

m

m

UNIT I   Let's Read! • **Lesson 12** *The Chase*

▶ Listening for Consonants

Directions: Write *m* in the first space if the picture starts with /m/.
Write *m* in the second space if the picture ends with /m/.

   m _____

   _____ m

   m _____

   _____ m

   _____ m

   _____ m

   m _____

   _____ m

UNIT 1 **Let's Read! • Lesson 13** *Mrs. Goose's Baby*

Sounds and Spellings

Directions: Practice writing a and A. Then write your name in the blank in the first sentence and write a word or draw a picture to complete the second sentence.

a

a a a a a a a a

A A A A A A A A

I am Answers will vary.

I am in a Answers will vary.

UNIT 1   **Let's Read!** • **Lesson 13** *Mrs. Goose's Baby*

▶ Reading and Writing

I am in the

I am in the

I am a _____.

I am in the

I am on the

I am a _____.

I am on the

I am in the

I am a _____.

Phonics Skills • *Decoding*   **UNIT 1** • **Lesson 13**   **19**

▶ Sounds and Spellings

Directions: Practice writing *t* and *T*. Then copy the words.

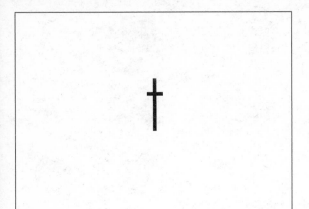

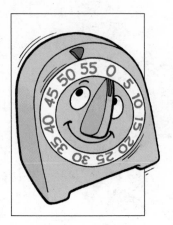

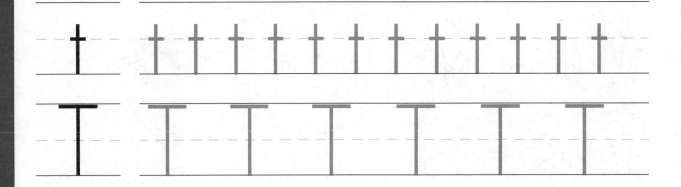

▶ Writing Words

at at   mat mat

Consonant Sounds and Spellings • **Phonics Skills**

Listening for Consonants

Directions: Write *t* on the first line if the picture begins with /t/ and write *t* on the second line if the picture ends with /t/.

_____
t
_____

_____
t
_____

_____
          t
_____

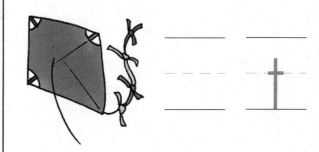

_____
          t
_____

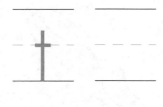

t
_____
_____

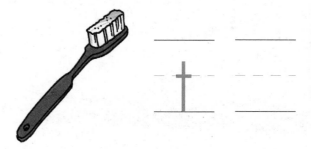

_____
t
_____

_____
          t
_____

_____
t   t
_____

▶ Sounds and Spellings

Directions: Practice writing *h* and *H*. Complete the sentences by writing words for the pictures.

h_

h   h h h h h h h h h h

H   H H H H H H H H

▶ Completing Sentences

A tam is a **hat**.

Matt has a **ham**.

▶ Listening for Consonants

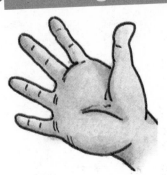

h   h   _____

_____   _____   h

_____   h   h

► # Sounds and Spellings

Directions: Practice writing *p* and *P*. Then copy the words and the sentence.

p p p p p p p p p p p p

P P P P P P P P P

► ## Writing Words and Sentences

pat pat   tap tap

Pam has a map.

Pam has a map.

Pat has a hat.
Pam is at the map.

Pam is at the map.

I tap the hat.
Pat is on a mat.

Pat is on a mat.

I tap the mat.
Pat has a hat.

Pat has a hat.

Directions: Practice writing *i* and *I*. Then copy the words and the sentence.

Sounds and Spellings

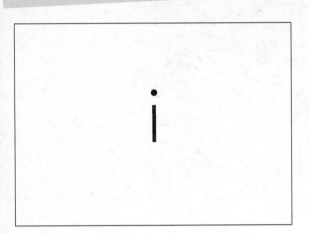

i

I

Writing Words and Sentences

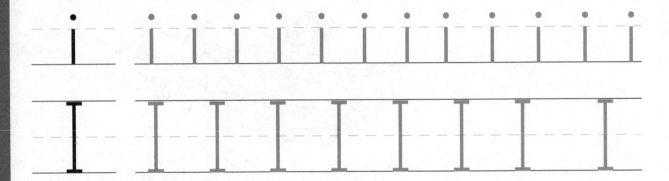

him him   tips tips

Tim sits in the pit.

Tim sits in the pit.

UNIT 2   Animals • **Lesson 2** *Raccoons*

▶ Writing Words

 ___ pit

 hip

hats

___ sits

Phonics Skills • *Blending*

▷ Sounds and Spellings

n

n n n n n n n n n

N N N N N N N N

▷ Writing Words and Sentences

nap nap   man man

Nan has a nap.

Nan has a nap.

Consonant Sounds and Spellings • Phonics Skills

Directions: Practice writing *n* and *N*. Then copy the words and the sentence.

UNIT 2 Animals • **Lesson 3** *Baby Animals*

▶ Completing Sentences

Directions: Look at the pictures and complete the sentences with the appropriate words.

 Pam has a __hat__.

| hat |
| nap |

 Pat has a __map__.

| pan |
| map |

 The ant is on the __ham__.

| ham |
| hat |

 Nat has a __pan__.

| nap |
| pan |

▶ Dictation

_____ pan _____   _____ nap _____

Name _____ Date _____

▷ Sounds and Spellings

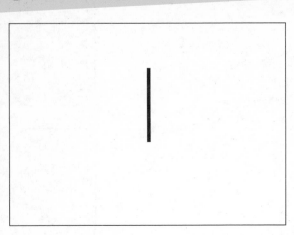

I

l | | | | | | | | | |

L | L | L | L | L | L | L

▷ Writing Words and Sentences

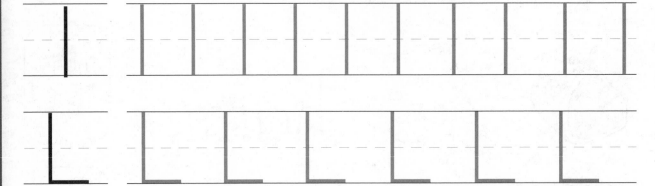

last last   hill hill

Hal has the last list.

Hal has the last list.

UNIT 2 Animals • **Lesson 4** *Baby Animals*

▶ Completing Sentences

last
list

Lil makes a ___list___.

lit
lap

Hal ___lit___ the lamp.

▶ **Review**

Directions: Choose the word that matches each picture, and write the word in the space provided.

| list | map | stamp | spill | ham | hat |

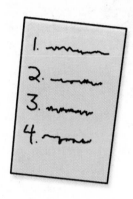

stamp   list   hat

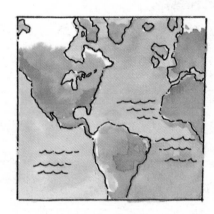

spill   map   ham

Decoding • **Phonics Skills**

▶ **Completing Sentences**

Directions: Look at the pictures and finish the sentences with the appropriate words.

Tim has a map .

| map |
| nap |

Sam makes a spill .

| spin |
| spill |

▶ **Dictation**

lap

lip

nap

tan

Sounds and Spellings

Directions: Practice writing *d* and *D*. Then copy the words and the sentence.

d

d d d d d d d d d d

D D D D D D D D

Writing Words and Sentences

dad dad   mad mad

Dad had a hat.

Dad had a hat.

UNIT 2   Animals • **Lesson 6** *Munch Crunch*

▶ **Reading and Writing**

Directions: Circle the word or sentence that matches each picture. Then write the word or sentence on the line.

hat

(hand)

pan

hand

nap

map

(Dad)

Dad

(Dad has a pan.)

Dad can nap.

Dad can pat the sand.

Dad has a pan.

Sounds and Spellings

Directions: Practice writing o and O. Then write the word that matches each picture and copy the sentence.

O   O O O O O O O O

O   O O O O O O

Writing Words and Sentences

   mop

   pot

Dot can stop the top.

Dot can stop the top.

Vowel Sounds and Spellings • **Phonics Skills**

UNIT 2   Animals • **Lesson 7** *Munch Crunch*

Completing Sentences ▶

Directions: Complete the sentences with the appropriate word.

Dad can spin a **top** .

| tap |
| tip |
| top |

Pam and Sam **pat** Spot.

| pat |
| pit |
| pot |

The pot is **hot** .

| hat |
| hit |
| hot |

Dictation ▶

top   hot

pot   spot

Name _____ Date _____

▶ Sounds and Spellings

b   b b b b b b b b b

B   B B B B B B

▶ Writing Words and Sentences

bib bib bands bands

A bat was a bit sad.

A bat was a bit sad.

Directions: Practice writing *b* and *B*. Then copy the words and the sentence.

Directions: Circle the word or sentence that matches each picture. Then write the word or sentence on the line.

bat

bats

bit

bats

pin

pit

pan

pin

Sid sat in the sand.

Nan and Sid had a pin.

Nan and Sid had a pin.

Sounds and Spellings

Directions: Practice writing c and C. Then copy the words and the sentence.

c

c c c c c c c c c c c

C C C C C C C C

Writing Words and Sentences

cat _cat_   cap _cap_

Can the cat tap on the can?

Can the cat tap on the can?

▶ **Writing Words**

Directions: Write the word for each picture under the picture. Then choose words from under the pictures to complete the sentences.

cat   map   cap

Nan can pat the cat .

Pam has a map .

▶ **Dictation**

cap

cot

can

cop

Phonics Skills • *Decoding/Dictation*

▶ **Review**

Directions: Write the word from the box that goes with each picture.

| hand | cat | pan | mop | band | pin |

mop

band

pin

pan

cat

hand

Decoding • Phonics Skills

▶ **Completing Sentences**

Dan has a ___cat___.

| cap |
| cat |

Pat has a ___mop___.

| mop |
| mitt |

Bob has a ___band___.

| hand |
| band |

UNIT 2 Animals • **Lesson II** *Spiders*

▶ Sounds and Spellings

Directions: Form words by blending the consonants in the box with _ack, _ick, and _ock.

c

☐ ck

| s | st | p | t |

_ack _ick _ock

sack	sick	sock
stack	stick	stock
pack	pick	pock
tack	tick	tock

▶ **Reading and Writing**

Mack packs a snack.
Stan stacks the sticks.

Directions: Write the sentence that describes the picture.

Mack packs a

snack.

▶ **Dictation**

sack   snack

pick   pack

▶ Sounds and Spellings

r

r r r r r r r r r r r

R R R R R R R R R

▶ Writing Words and Sentences

rip rip   trip trip

A cat ran past the rat.

A cat ran past the rat.

Directions: Practice writing r and R. Then copy the words and the sentence.

▶ **Reading and Writing**

Brad ran on the ramp.
The rabbit is in the crib.

The rabbit is in the

crib.

Min ran at camp.
Tim is on a trip.

Min ran at camp.

Sid stands in the sand.
Sid can stand on his hands.

Sid can stand on

his hands.

▶ Sounds and Spellings

u   u   U   u   u   u   u

U   U   U   U   U   U   U   U

▶ Writing Words and Sentences

bud bud drum drum

The duck is stuck in the mud.

The duck is stuck in
the mud.

Directions: Practice writing *u* and *U*. Then copy the words and the sentence.

▶ **Reading and Writing**

Directions: Copy the sentence that describes each picture.

Pam scrubs the pup's hut.
Pam has a pup.

Pam has a pup.

Bud is in the sun.
The mutt runs up the pump.

Bud is in the sun.

▶ **Dictation**

bun   run

nut   cut

Sid and Sam run.

Sounds and Spellings

Directions: Practice writing *g* and *G*. Then copy the words and the sentence.

g

g   g g g g g g g g g g g g

G   G G G G G G

Writing Words and Sentences

gas gas   grab grab

The pig is big.

The pig is big.

UNIT 2   Animals • **Lesson 14** *The Hermit Crab*

▶ Writing Words

pig

sag

grin

_____   _____
pig   grin

tag

dig

big

_____   _____
tag   big

Directions: Write the words represented in the picture.

▶ **Review**

Directions: Look at each picture and complete each sentence with the appropriate word.

Rod sat on a rock .

| dock |
| rock |

Bob has a bug .

| bug |
| rug |

Rob has a stick .

| stick |
| pick |

Decoding • **Phonics Skills**

► **Writing Words**

| bag | duck | pig |

duck   bag   pig

► **Dictation**

big   had

tub   not

The rock is big.

Directions: Write the word from the box that goes with each picture.

Directions: Practice writing *j* and *J*. Then copy the words and the sentence in the spaces provided.

► Sounds and Spellings

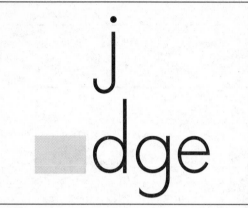

j

J

► Writing Words and Sentences

job job judge judge

just just badge badge

Jack sat on a bridge.

Jack sat on a bridge.

Consonant Sounds and Spellings • Phonics Skills

▶ **Reading and Writing**

Directions: Copy the sentence that matches the picture.

> Jack jogs on the bridge.
> Jan jumps on the bridge.

Jack jogs on the

bridge.

▶ **Dictation**

jog   jump

job   jam

The ant is on the

cap.

▶ Sounds and Spellings

Directions: Practice writing *f* and *F*. Then copy the words and the sentence in the spaces provided.

f

f f f f f f f f f f f f f

F F F F F F F F F

▶ Writing Words and Sentences

fan fan   fat fat

Can the fat cat fit in the hat?

Can the fat cat fit in the hat?

Consonant Sounds and Spellings • **Phonics Skills**

Writing Words

Directions: Write the letter or sound represented by each *Sound/Spelling Card* picture to form a word.

fit

trip

   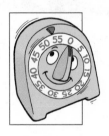

fast

ramp

Phonics Skills • *Blending*

Sounds and Spellings

Directions: Practice writing e and E. Then copy the words and the sentence in the spaces provided.

e

e e e e e e e e e e e

E E E E E E E E

Writing Words and Sentences

hen hen tent tent

neck neck sled sled

The egg is in a bed.

The egg is in a bed.

UNIT 3   **Things That Go • Lesson 3** *I Go With My Family to Grandma's*

▶ **Writing Words**

Directions: Write the name of each picture.

 fan

 hen

 pen

 pan

 men

 man

▶ **Dictation**

pen

ten

tent

end

Ben has a red hen.

▶ **Review**

bridge	bell	sled	leg	ball	fell

ball   bell   fell

leg   bridge   sled

Listening for Consonants

Directions: Write the name of each picture beneath the consonant that is contained in that word.

l	f
bell	fan
doll	gift
lamp	raft

Sounds and Spellings

Directions: Practice writing x and X. Then copy the words and the sentence in the spaces provided.

x   x   x   x   x   x   x   x   x   x   x   x

X   X   X   X   X   X   X   X

Writing Words and Sentences

fox fox   mix mix

The ax is in the box.

The ax is in the box.

▶ **Listening for Vowels**

__o__

__fox__

__a__

__bag__

__i__

__six__

▶ **Dictation**

six

fig

box

bag

Tom can fix
the cab.

Directions: Write the name of each picture beneath the short-vowel spelling contained in the word.

Sounds and Spellings

z

__s

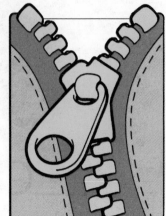

Directions: Practice writing z and Z. Then copy the words and the sentence in the spaces provided.

z z z z z z z z z z

Z Z Z Z Z Z Z Z Z Z

Writing Words and Sentences

zip zip   buzz buzz

He ran in a zigzag.

He ran in a zigzag.

UNIT 3   **Things That Go • Lesson 6** *Song of the Train*

> ### ▶ Writing Words

Pam   pup   robin   rat

rat's    pup's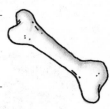

Pam's    robin's

pot   man   cat   fox

pot's    cat's

fox's    man's

Phonics Skills • *Possessives*   **UNIT 3 • Lesson 6**   **65**

▷ **Review**

box	fan	fox	grass	press	zip

fox   press   fan

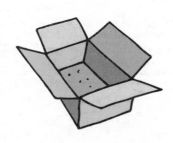

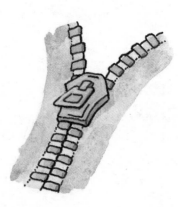

grass   box   zip

Decoding • Phonics Skills

UNIT 3   Things That Go • **Lesson 7** *Song of the Train*

Completing Sentences

Directions: Look at the pictures and finish the sentences with the appropriate word.

Pam makes a **mess**.

moss
mess

Sam will **toss** a rock.

toss
boss

Dictation

jug   jazz

flag   flat

The pig jumped in the pond.

Sounds and Spellings

Directions: Copy the words and the sentence in the spaces provided.

sh

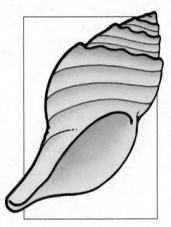

Writing Words and Sentences

shop shop rash rash

mash mash lash lash

Trish has six shells in a box.

Trish has six shells

in a box.

Writing Words

Directions: Write the word that goes with each picture. Then write the spelling represented by each **Sound/Spelling Card** picture to form a word at the bottom.

| dish | ship | shop | shell | brush | fish |

shell

fish

shop

ship

brush

dish

sh   e   l   f

Directions: Copy the words and the sentence in the spaces provided.

► Sounds and Spellings

th

► Writing Words and Sentences

thin *thin*   that *that*

math *math*   bath *bath*

thump *thump*

This is a thick cloth.

This is a thick cloth.

Name _____ Date _____

▶ **Unscrambling Sentences**

Directions: Unscramble the words to form a sentence that describes the picture.

| slips | the | Bill | on | mud. |

Bill slips on the mud.

▶ **Dictation**

shop   them

that   flash

Dad had a ship.

▶ Review

th
sh

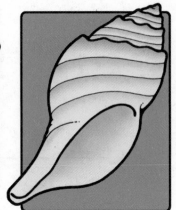

Directions: Copy the words and the sentence on the lines provided.

▶ Writing Words and Sentences

thick   thick   than   than

trash   trash   shop   shop

bath   bath   shut   shut

She left the trash in the shop.

She left the trash
in the shop.

▶ Listening for Consonants

Directions: Name each picture. Write the name of each picture beneath the consonant sound contained in that word.

sh	th
ship	bath
shell	path
dish	math

Sounds and Spellings

ch
■tch

Writing Words and Sentences

fetch   fetch   rich   rich

ditch   ditch   chin   chin

Mitch can catch the pitch.

Mitch can catch the

pitch.

► **Writing Words**

Directions: Write the word that goes with each picture.

| fetch | patches | crutches | catch | ditch | bench |

bench   catch   crutches

► **Dictation**

chip   chimp

ditch   pitch

Tim chats with Mitch.

Name ——————————— Date ———————

UNIT 3 **Things That Go • Lesson 12** *On the Go*

Sounds and Spellings

ar

Writing Words and Sentences

 car　　 barn

 star　　 card

The car is in the barn.

The car is in the barn.

Directions: Write the ar word next to each picture. Then copy the sentence.

76 UNIT 3 • Lesson 12   *Vowel Sounds and Spellings* • Phonics Skills

UNIT 3 **Things That Go • Lesson 12** *On the Go*

▶ **Writing Words**

Directions: Look at the picture. Write the words in the list that appear in the picture. Then name other objects in the picture. Circle the words with the /ar/ sound.

(car)

(star)

ram

(barn)

man

rabbit

frog

ax

(car)

(star)

(barn)

man

rabbit

ax

fox

cat

rat

dog

bugs

pan

Phonics Skills • *Decoding*

▶ **Review**

Directions: Write the word that goes with each picture.

| mug | fox | tent | bag | pin | nut |

tent   nut   mug

pin   bag   fox

UNIT 3 **Things That Go • Lesson 13** *Trucks (Camiones)*

Completing Sentences

Directions: Look at the pictures and complete the sentences with the appropriate words.

 Dan has a pet fish .

| frog |
| fish |

 Nan's dog can fetch .

| fetch |
| match |

Dictation

at   tug

had   step

Dan will pitch the

trash in the can.

Sounds and Spellings

Directions: Practice writing w and W. Then copy the words and the sentence in the spaces provided.

W_

w   w   w   w   w   w   w

W   W   W   W   W   W   W

Writing Words and Sentences

wet wet   wag wag

win win   well well

Will won a wagon.

Will won a wagon.

Directions: Copy the words and the sentence in the spaces provided.

▶ **Sounds and Spellings**

wh_

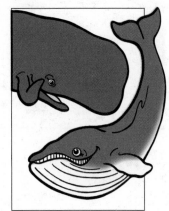

▶ **Writing Words and Sentences**

when when

whip whip

When will Jim whip the mix?

When will Jim whip

the mix?

Directions: Copy the words and sentence in the spaces provided.

► **Sounds and Spellings**

er
ir
ur

► **Writing Words and Sentences**

her her   bird bird

girl girl   fern fern

curl curl   turn turn

Bert had a burger for supper.

Bert had a burger

for supper.

► **Unscrambling Sentences**

> has   girl   a
> The   turtle.

The girl has a turtle.

► **Dictation**

wet   went

girl   turn

Her cat had

wet fur.

Directions: Unscramble the words to form a sentence that describes the picture.

▶ Review

| turtle | bird | catch | girl | wag | wig |

wig   catch   bird

turtle   wag   girl

▶ **Completing Sentences**

Directions: Look at the pictures and complete the sentences with the correct words.

Bob has a pet bird .

| turtle |
| bird |

Pat has a red wagon .

| wagon |
| dragon |

▶ **Dictation**

batch   patch

will   went

I will catch a

small bird.

Sounds and Spellings

Directions: Practice writing *k* and *K*. Then copy the words and the sentence in the spaces provided.

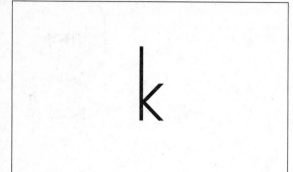

k   k   k   k   k   k   k   k

K   K   K   K   K   K   K   K

Writing Words and Sentences

kick   kick   bark   bark

silk   silk   kettle   kettle

The kitten laps milk.

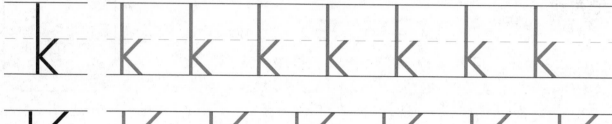

The kitten laps milk.

▶ **Writing Words**

Directions: Write the word that goes with each picture.

| park | milk | skirt | mask | skillet | kettle |

kettle   mask   park

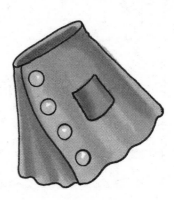

milk   skillet   skirt

Sounds and Spellings

ng

Writing Words and Sentences

sing   <u>sing</u>   thing   <u>thing</u>

ring   <u>ring</u>   wing   <u>wing</u>

He rang a gong.

He rang a gong.

We sang a song.

We sang a song.

Directions: Copy the words and the sentences in the spaces provided.

▶ **Reading and Writing**

Directions: Write the sentence described by each picture.

The string is tangled.
The string is in a box.

The string is in a box.

He swung at the ball.
He plays on the swing.

He swung at the ball.

▶ **Dictation**

bring   string

Hank   bank

Hank will bring a dog.

▶ Sounds and Spellings

qu_

Directions: Practice writing *qu* and *Qu*. Then copy the words and the sentence in the spaces provided.

qu   qu qu qu qu qu

Qu   Qu Qu Qu Qu

▶ Writing Words and Sentences

quilt   quilt   quit   quit

quick   quick   quiz   quiz

The quilt has stars.

The quilt has stars.

UNIT 4   **Our Neighborhood at Work • Lesson 4** *Guess Who?*

▶ Listening for Words

Directions: Read the words in the boxes. Then choose the correct word based on the clues given.

● quit	○ market	○ liquid
○ quick	○ check	● licked
○ quilt	● quack	○ locked

● squint	● quill	○ squirt
○ squirm	○ king	○ squint
○ squiggle	○ kick	● squish

Name _____ Date _____

► Sounds and Spellings

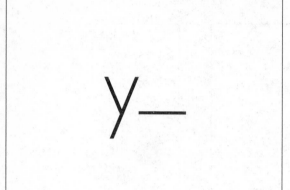

y —

y y y y y y y y y y y y

Y Y Y Y Y Y Y Y Y Y

► Writing Words and Sentences

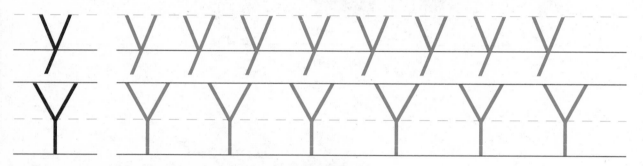

yarn yarn   yes yes

yell yell   yet yet

The yak likes yams.

The yak likes yams.

Directions: Practice writing y and Y. Then copy the words and the sentence in the spaces provided.

▶ **Reading and Writing**

Directions: Write the sentence that matches the picture.

> The dog yelps at the rabbit.
> A rabbit nibbles plants in the yard.
> The dog naps in the backyard.

The dog yelps at
the rabbit.

▶ **Dictation**

yes   yet

yard   yarn

The pups yelp for
help.

▶ Review

ring	yarn	kitten	yak	skunk	quilt

yak   ring   skunk

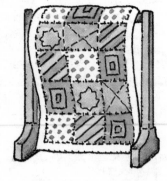

quilt   yarn   kitten

▶ **Completing Sentences**

Directions: Look at the pictures and complete the sentences with the appropriate word.

Nan has a __ring__ on her finger.

rat
ring

We can smell a __skunk__.

trunk
skunk

The kitten has the __yarn__.

yarn
barn

Phonics Skills • *Decoding*

Name _____ Date _____

▶ **Sounds and Spellings**

a
a_e

▶ **Writing Words and Sentences**

ape   <u>ape</u>

cane   <u>cane</u>

late   <u>late</u>

Dale made a mask with paper and tape.

<u>Dale made a mask</u>

<u>with paper and tape.</u>

Directions: Copy the words and the sentence in the spaces provided.

UNIT 4 **Our Neighborhood at Work • Lesson 7** *Firefighters*

▶ **Completing Sentences**

Directions: Complete each sentence with the appropriate word.

1. Ted is a ___man___ .

2. Pat fixed his model ___plane___ .

3. A whale ___can___ swim.

| man |
| mane |

| plan |
| plane |

| can |
| cane |

▶ **Dictation**

ate   gate

rake   brake

Jake made a cake.

Phonics Skills • *Decoding/Dictation*

▶ Sounds and Spellings

s
ce
ci__

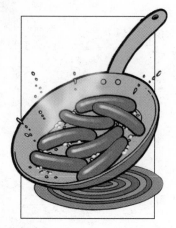

▶ Writing Words and Sentences

cent   <u>cent</u>   cell   <u>cell</u>

circle   <u>circle</u>

Grace has six cents.

<u>Grace has six cents.</u>

The girls danced.

<u>The girls danced.</u>

▶ **Listening for Consonants**

Directions: List each word under the **Sound/Spelling Card** picture for /s/ or /k/.

face	cake	race	candle
picnic	carrot	lace	space

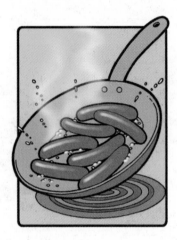

face

race

lace

space

cake

candle

picnic

carrot

▶ **Review**

Directions: Write the word that goes with each picture.

| cake   tape   rake   ape   face   plane |

rake

face

ape

plane

cake

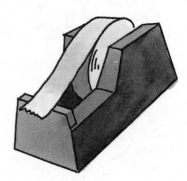

tape

Name ______________________________ Date ____________

Writing Words

Directions: Use the letters to make word families.

b c m

___ake bake cake make

sh c dr

___ape shape cape drape

Dictation

lace place

cinder circle

I had two cents to spend.

► **Sounds and Spellings**

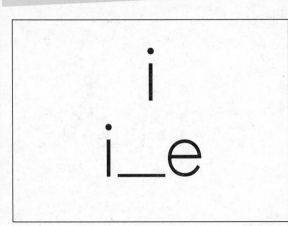
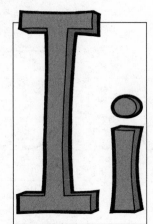

► **Writing Words and Sentences**

tiger tiger title title

time time mile mile

Nine fish swim.

Nine fish swim.

Did he find a dime?

Did he find a dime?

Directions: Copy the words and the sentences in the spaces provided.

UNIT 4   Our Neighborhood at Work • **Lesson 10** *Firefighters*

Completing Sentences

Directions: Complete each sentence with the appropriate word.

1. I like to **ride** _____ my bike.

| rid |
| ride |

2. Did you **rip** _____ the paper?

| rip |
| ripe |

3. Dad made a **fine** _____ dinner.

| fin |
| fine |

4. The man did a **kind** _____ act.

| kin |
| kind |

5. The lamp is **dim** _____ .

| dim |
| dime |

6. Do not let the dog **bite** _____ .

| bit |
| bite |

▶ Sounds and Spellings

o
o__e

▶ Writing Words and Sentences

Directions: Copy the words and the sentences in the spaces provided.

no   no   rode   rode

hold   hold   stone   stone

The dog hid a bone.

The dog hid a bone.

I broke the pole.

I broke the pole.

▶ **Listening for Words**

Directions: Read the words in the boxes, then choose the correct word based on the clues given.

○ April	○ hop	○ block
● open	○ hope	○ bone
○ omit	● hold	● broke

▶ **Dictation**

go   hope

hold   open

Stan told us a

joke.

Review

| cradle   rake   snake   table   lake   tape |

snake   tape   cradle

table   lake   rake

▶ **Completing Sentences**

Directions: Look at each picture and complete each sentence with the correct word.

A <u>snake</u> is in the grass.

snack
snake

The candle has a <u>flame</u>.

flame
plan

Bill can <u>tape</u> the rip.

tape
tap

▶ **Review**

Directions: Look at the pictures and complete each sentence with the correct word.

The ducks swam in the lake.

| lock |
| lake |

Brett ate a dish of rice.

| rice |
| race |

Jane ate a big cone.

| bone |
| cone |

▶ **Writing Words**

| nine | rope | tape |

Directions: Write the word that goes with each picture.

rope   tape   nine

▶ **Dictation**

cargo   banjo

label   silent

I'd like to go on

a spaceship.

Phonics Skills • *Decoding/Dictation*   **UNIT 4 • Lesson 13** **109**

Directions: Practice writing v and V. Then copy the words and the sentence in the spaces provided.

▶ Sounds and Spellings

v

v v v v v v v v v

V V V V V V V V V

▶ Writing Words and Sentences

vine vine van van

brave brave five five

Viv has a valentine.

Viv has a valentine.

▶ **Completing Sentences**

Directions: Complete each sentence with the appropriate word.

| stove | drives | never |
| velvet | saves | vase |

1. My mom <u>drives</u> a van.

2. Jim <u>saves</u> baseball cards.

3. Jan has a <u>velvet</u> dress.

4. Lance put the pan on the <u>stove</u>.

5. Put the buds in a <u>vase</u>.

Sounds and Spellings

u

u_e

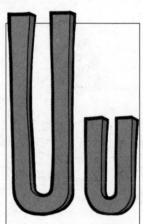

Writing Words and Sentences

fuse fuse cute cute

cube cube use use

The mule likes music.

The mule likes music.

Cole has cute cats.

Cole has cute cats.

Vowel Sounds and Spellings • **Phonics Skills**

▶ **Reading and Writing**

Directions: Write the sentence described by the picture.

The mule has a cute hat.
The mule licks an ice cube.

The mule has a

cute hat.

▶ **Dictation**

unit   human

use   fuse

Judy likes to hum

music.

Sounds and Spellings

j ge
   gi_

Writing Words and Sentences

gem _gem_   rage _rage_

just _just_   page _page_

The gerbil ran into the cage.

The gerbil ran into
the cage.

▶ **Completing Sentences**

Directions: Complete each sentence with the correct word.

1. Kate has a _____bag_____ of games.

| bag |
| bridge |

2. Tim _____gave_____ a gift to Kim.

| gave |
| gentle |

3. We had a play on the _____stage_____.

| joke |
| stage |

▶ **Dictation**

ginger   huge

engine   gem

Dan put ginger in the cake.

▶ Sounds and Spellings

e

e__e

Directions: Copy the words and the sentences in the spaces provided.

▶ Writing Words and Sentences

we <u>we</u>   even <u>even</u>

he <u>he</u>   she <u>she</u>

Peter ran after me.

<u>Peter ran after me.</u>

I had a fever today.

<u>I had a fever today.</u>

Reading and Writing

Directions: Write the sentence that tells about each picture.

She runs ten meters.
She runs a fever.

She runs ten meters.

Steve has a fever.
Steve ate these eggs.

Steve has a fever.

She is on a trapeze.
She mixes concrete.

She mixes concrete.

▶ Review

| bridge | music | she | cage | vine | mule |

cage

she

music

mule

bridge

vine

Sounds and Spellings • **Phonics Skills**

UNIT 5 • **Weather** • **Lesson 3** *When a Storm Comes Up*

▶ **Completing Sentences**

Directions: Look at the pictures and complete each sentence with the correct word.

Sue sang on the __stage__.

bridge   stage

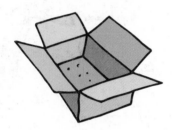

The box was __large__.

large   judge

▶ **Dictation**

be   behind

these   use

Pete has a secret.

▶ **Review**

Directions: Write the word that goes with each picture.

> cake   jump   athlete   mice   she   mule

jump

she

mule

mice

cake

athlete

▶ Completing Sentences

She ————— got first prize.

He
She

The bird ————— is in the cage.

bird
brim

The wall is made of concrete .

dirt
concrete

Directions: Copy the words and the sentences in the spaces provided.

▶ Sounds and Spellings

ee
ea

▶ Writing Words and Sentences

real   real   meal   meal

feel   feel   sheep   sheep

He eats green beans.

He eats green beans.

The seal fell asleep.

The seal fell asleep.

UNIT 5 Weather • **Lesson 5** *When a Storm Comes Up*

▶ **Writing Opposites**

| begin | awake | fake | end | real | asleep |

begin   end

awake   asleep

fake   real

▶ **Dictation**

mean   stream

see   need

The seal eats fish.

Phonics Skills • *Antonyms*   UNIT 5 • Lesson 5 **123**

▶ Sounds and Spellings

_y
_ie_

Directions: Copy the words and the sentences in the spaces provided.

▶ Writing Words and Sentences

chief chief city city

pony pony tiny tiny

Betty saves pennies.

Betty saves pennies.

Sally fed the bunnies.

Sally fed the bunnies.

UNIT 5   Weather • **Lesson 6** *Listen to the Rain*

▶ **Reading and Writing**

The lily is white.
The lilies are white.

The lilies are white.

The box is shiny.
The box is dirty.

The box is shiny.

The puppy is sleepy.
Puppies are sleepy.

Puppies are sleepy.

The pony runs away.
The thief runs away.

The pony runs away.

Phonics Skills • *Decoding*   UNIT 5 • Lesson 6   **125**

Directions: Write the word that goes with each picture.

tire	cheer	shore	hear	square	core

core   shore   square

cheer   tire   hear

Completing Sentences

Amy _____ **wore** _____ a dress.

tore   wore

Pups _____ **stare** _____ at a bug.

stare   steer

Dictation

here   hire

scare   score

I got wire at a store.

Directions: Look at the pictures and complete each sentence with the correct word.

▶ **Sounds and Spellings**

ai__
__ay

▶ **Writing Words and Sentences**

Directions: Copy the words and the sentences in the spaces provided.

pail pail snail snail

pay pay stay stay

The raisins are stale.

The raisins are stale.

It is Kay's birthday.

It is Kay's birthday.

UNIT 5 • Weather • **Lesson 8** *How's the Weather?*

Writing Words

nail   pail

pail

sail   hail

sail

mail   tail

tail

may   mail

mail

way   waste

waste

plane   play

plane

▶ Sounds and Spellings

igh

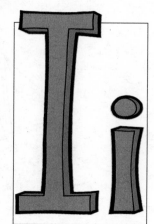

▶ Writing Words and Sentences

high   high   sigh   sigh

sight   sight   flight   flight

The light is bright.

The light is bright.

You might be right.

You might be right.

Name ______________________ Date __________

Writing Words

Directions: Use the words in the left column with the words in the right column to make compound words.

light	cut
hair	rope
tight	bulb

lightbulb

haircut

tightrope

Dictation

high bright

paint stay

It rained day and night.

► **Review**

dime	stone	tree	smile	puppy	bone

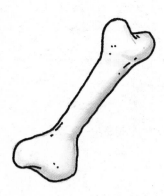

bone

tree

stone

dime

puppy

smile

UNIT 5   **Weather • Lesson 10** *Clouds, Rain, Snow, and Ice*

▶ **Completing Sentences**

Directions: Look at the pictures and complete each sentence with the correct word.

She smelled the <u>rose</u>.

bows
rose

Jane went to the <u>beach</u>.

park
beach

Dan broke his <u>nose</u>.

nose
toes

Phonics Skills • *Decoding*   **UNIT 5 • Lesson 10**   **133**

▶ Sounds and Spellings

_y
_ie

▶ Writing Words and Sentences

Directions: Copy the words and the sentences in the spaces provided.

try <u>try</u>   tries <u>tries</u>

fly <u>fly</u>   flies <u>flies</u>

Birds fly in the sky.

<u>Birds fly in the sky.</u>

He tries the pie.

<u>He tries the pie.</u>

UNIT 5 **Weather • Lesson 11** *Good Day for Kites*

▶ **Completing Sentences**

| fly | tie | tries | pie | sky |

Directions: Write the correct word in each blank.

1. The __fly__ buzzes past my head.

2. I ate the apple __pie__ all by myself.

3. Tyrone __tries__ to do a trick.

▶ **Dictation**

light   fry

lady   ladies

Patty likes pies.

Phonics Skills • *Decoding/Dictation*   UNIT 5 • Lesson 11   **135**

Sounds and Spellings

_oe

Writing Words and Sentences

Directions: Copy the words and the sentences in the spaces provided.

no   no   doe   doe

toe   toe   Joe   Joe

Joe will hoe the garden.

Joe will hoe the

garden.

Listening for Words

● oboe	● Joe	○ block
● open	● joke	● bone
● oval	○ job	● broke

○ too	○ not	● go
● toe	● no	○ got
● tone	● nose	● gold

 n

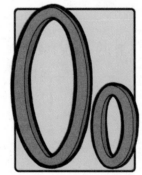 o

A worm has no feet.

Directions: Copy the words and the sentences in the spaces provided.

Sounds and Spellings

o
oa__

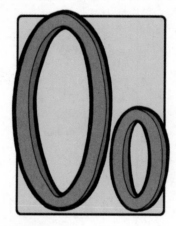

Writing Words and Sentences

_____   _____

soap <u>soap</u> oat <u>oat</u>

A toad ate my toast.

<u>A toad ate my toast.</u>

Joan had a coat at the coast.

<u>Joan had a coat</u>

<u>at the coast.</u>

▶ Sounds and Spellings

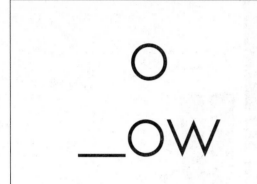
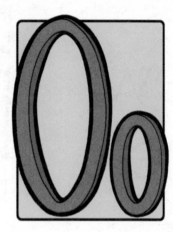

○
_ow

▶ Writing Words

grow grow   row row

▶ Dictation

gold   grow

snowing   saying

Joe rows a boat.

Phonics Skills • *Vowel Sounds and Spellings*   UNIT 5 • Lesson 13   **139**

▶ **Sounds and Spellings**

u_ew
_ue

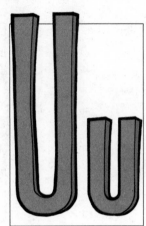

Uu

▶ **Writing Words and Sentences**

few <u>few</u> cue <u>cue</u>

pew <u>pew</u> hue <u>hue</u>

The firefighter rescued the cat.

<u>The firefighter</u>

<u>rescued the cat.</u>

Directions: Copy the words and the sentence in the spaces provided.

Completing Sentences

Directions: Fill in the blank with the correct word.

use	mule	amuse	rescue	few

1. He will **rescue** the cat from the tree.

2. We rode a **mule** down the trail.

3. There are only a **few** seconds left.

4. The puppet will **amuse** you.

5. You can **use** a hammer and nails to make it.

▶ **Review**

Directions: Write the word that goes with each picture.

| fly | boat | pie | toe | coat | bow |

boat

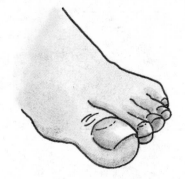

toe

fly

bow

pie

coat

Decoding • **Phonics Skills**

▶ **Completing Sentences**

Directions: Look at the picture and finish the sentence with the correct word.

_____

The snow fell outside.

rain

snow

▶ **Dictation**

mew   few

cue   argue

There are a few

music stores.

Sounds and Spellings

oo   u_e
_ue _ew
u

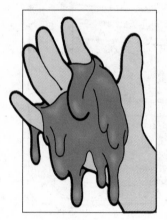

Writing Words and Sentences

food   food   flute   flute

glue   glue   tuba   tuba

The balloon floats up to the moon.

The balloon floats

up to the moon.

Directions: Copy the words and the sentence in the spaces provided.

▶ **Writing Words**

Directions: Circle the word in each sentence with the /ōō/ sound. Then write the words in the spaces provided.

1. He huffed and he puffed and he (blew) it down.

blew

2. The farmer's (goose) honked at me.

goose

3. I saw a (cocoon) on a leaf.

cocoon

4. She made a nest for (bluebirds).

bluebirds

5. Do you have the (rules) of the game?

rules

▶ **Dictation**

rude   true

chew   booth

Sue has a new tooth.

Name _____ Date _____

Sounds and Spellings

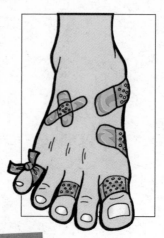

oo

Writing Words and Sentences

brook brook

hood hood

Ed shook his foot.

Ed shook his foot.

I took the book.

I took the book.

Directions: Copy the words and the sentences in the spaces provided.

► **Reading and Writing**

Directions: Write the sentence described by each picture.

Ned has a hood.
Ned chops wood.

Ned has a hood.

Susan reads a book.
Susan tries to cook.

Susan tries to cook.

Tom hangs his coat on a hook.
Tom sits by a brook.

Tom sits by a brook.

▶ **Review**

| goose | balloon | moon | flute | stew | moose |

flute   moon   balloon

goose   stew   moose

► **Writing Words**

Directions: Complete each sentence with the correct word.

Karen <u>drew</u> a picture.

stew
drew

Tonya used <u>glue</u> for her project.

glue
drew

► **Dictation**

<u>look</u>   <u>hook</u>

<u>cook</u>   <u>took</u>

<u>Hop on one foot, Sue.</u>

▶ Sounds and Spellings

Directions: Copy the words and the sentence in the spaces provided. Then write a rhyming word to finish the sentence.

ow

▶ Writing Words and Sentences

how how   now now

Take a towel to the shower.

Take a towel to
the shower.

A cow that was brown went to the town .

▶ **Writing Words**

Directions: Write the word described by each picture.

cat
cow
crow

cow

shower
tower
flower

flower

towel
owl
howl

owl

crown
gown
frown

crown

Sounds and Spellings

Directions: Copy the words and the sentences in the spaces provided.

ow
ou_

Writing Words and Sentences

out <u>out</u>   house <u>house</u>

A mouse ran out.

<u>A mouse ran out.</u>

The cloud is round.

<u>The cloud is round.</u>

UNIT 6 | **Journeys • Lesson 5** *Captain Bill Pinkney's Journey*

Completing Sentences

Directions: Complete each sentence with the correct word.

| how | snow | crow | crown | show |

1. The queen has a ___crown___ with a big round ruby.

2. Do you know ___how___ to play checkers?

3. The class put on a puppet ___show___ .

4. The ___snow___ made the ground white.

Dictation

found   cloud

sound   proud

We drove downtown.

Review

| clown | round | owl | crowd | towel | hound |

hound   clown   crowd

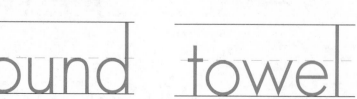

round   towel   owl

UNIT 6   Journeys • **Lesson 6** *Me on the Map*

Reading and Writing

"What do you like (about) parades?" asked Mom.

"I like the (sound) of drums," said Byron, "but I wish they weren't so (loud)."

"The (clowns) are funny," added Suzy. "One of them was walking slow and made the dog (growl)."

"I like to see the (crowd) wave and clap," said Dad.

"I know what I like," said Mom. "I like to hear the bands beat their drums and toot their horns."

Directions: Circle the words in the story with the /ow/ sound. Then write each word in the correct column.

ou

ow

ou	ow
sound	clowns
loud	growl
about	crowd

Phonics Skills • *Decoding*

Sounds and Spellings

aw

au_

Directions: Copy the words and the sentence in the spaces provided.

Writing Words and Sentences

raw raw   bawl bawl

pause pause

The baby crawls on the lawn.

The baby crawls

on the lawn.

▶ **Writing Words**

Directions: Look at the pictures and complete each sentence with the correct word.

_____

Paul put milk in the <u>saucer</u>.

shaker
saucer

<u>claw</u>

The hawk raised its <u>claw</u>.

straw
claw

▶ **Dictation**

saw   sauce

fawn   flaunt

The hound is brown.

▶ **Review**

Directions: Write the sentence that describes each picture.

Tim crawls across the carpet.
Tim pets the puppy.

Tim pets the puppy.

He ate a piece of straw.
She wore a shawl.

She wore a shawl.

A cow lies down.
A cow walked across town.

A cow lies down.

Decoding • **Phonics Skills**

UNIT 6 Journeys • **Lesson 8** *Me on the Map*

▶ **Word Study**

Directions: Circle the word in each row that does not rhyme with the other words.

how   cow   (crawl)   now

(lawn)   brown   town   crown

draw   (down)   saw   law

fawn   lawn   dawn   (shawl)

► Sounds and Spellings

$$\overset{n}{kn}\_$$

► Writing Words and Sentences

knit knit   knot knot

I know that knight.

I know that knight.

She knows how to knit.

She knows how

to knit.

Directions: Copy the words and the sentences in the spaces provided.

► **Writing Words**

Directions: Write the word that best completes each sentence.

| know | knock | knight | knee | knot |

1. Please __knock__ on the window.

2. She learned how to tie a __knot__.

3. Do you __know__ how to skate?

4. He hurt his __knee__ playing football.

► **Dictation**

know   knee

knead   knock

He knew the knight.

▶ **Review**

Directions: Write the word that goes with each picture.

cookie   hook   boot   spoon   book   cook

boot   cookie   cook

hook   spoon   book

▶ **Completing Sentences**

Directions: Look at the pictures and complete each sentence with the correct word.

The sweater is made of <u>wool</u>.

| wood |
| wool |

The wet puppy <u>shook</u>.

| shook |
| stood |

She read a <u>book</u>.

| boot |
| book |

Sounds and Spellings

Directions: Put the words in order from the least to the most. Use 1, 2, and 3.

2 sweeter

1 sweet

3 sweetest

3 highest

2 higher

1 high

1 cold

3 coldest

2 colder

2 harder

1 hard

3 hardest

▶ **Completing Sentences**

The sun is **brightest** of all.

bright   brighter   brightest

A pig has **shorter** legs than a sheep.

short   shorter   shortest

▶ **Dictation**

cool   cooler   coolest

hard   harder   hardest

My room is the coolest.

Directions: Look at the pictures and complete each sentence with the correct word.

Sounds and Spellings

oi

_oy

Directions: Copy the words and the sentence in the spaces provided.

Writing Words and Sentences

noise noise   joy joy

point point   toy toy

The boy has a nice voice.

The boy has a

nice voice.

► **Completing Sentences**

Directions: Complete each sentence with the correct word.

| coins | toy | noise | moist | point |

1. He got a _____toy_____ for his birthday.

2. The pencil has a _____point_____.

3. She collects _____coins_____.

4. The loud _____noise_____ woke us.

5. The cake was soft and _____moist_____.

Sounds and Spellings

r
wr_

Writing Words and Sentences

wrist wrist

wrap wrap

Robots wrestle rakes.

Robots wrestle rakes.

The boy wrote a note.

The boy wrote a note.

Directions: Copy the words and the sentences in the spaces provided.

► **Writing Words**

| write | wrench | wreath |

Directions: Write the word that goes with each picture.

wrench   write   wreath

► **Dictation**

write   wrote

quick   quilt

We wrote a quick note.

Sounds and Spellings

f
ph

Directions: Copy the words and the sentence in the spaces provided.

Writing Words and Sentences

photo   photo

trophy   trophy

Phil's nephew plays the saxophone.

Phil's nephew plays
the saxophone.

► **Writing Words**

trophy   elephant   dolphin   gopher

Directions: Write the word that goes with each picture.

trophy

gopher

dolphin

elephant

Phonics Skills • *Decoding*

Review

Directions: Write the correct word to complete each sentence.

| phone | wrote | boil | elephant | wrap |

1. I __wrote__ Grandma a letter.

2. The water on the stove will __boil__ .

3. Dad will __wrap__ the gift.

4. The __phone__ rang.

5. We saw an __elephant__ at the zoo.

UNIT 6   **Journeys • Lesson 15** *Unit Wrap-Up*

Word Study

1. wrap   wreath   (rake)   wrist

2. phone   photo   (farm)   elephant

3. (foam)   boil   soil   foil

4. voice   noise   (tube)   point

Dictation

wrap   wrist

cube   train

I write a letter

to my teacher.

Phonics Skills • *Decoding*   **UNIT 6 • Lesson 15   173**

Phonics   Circle the words with short vowel sounds.
Write them under the correct picture.

1. The boy dug in the mud.   3. He took a pen from the box.

2. Ben saw a big ram.   4. My dog likes ham.

ram

ham

in

big

Ben

pen

box

dog

dug

mud

▶ **Reading and Writing**

Circle the words with long vowel sounds.
Write them under the correct picture.

1. The bear was (huge.)

2. A (plane) was (high) in the (sky.)

3. Did Dad (read) the (mail?)

4. Will Pat (go) to the (store?)

5. (Pete) has a red (cube.)

Aa

plane

mail

Ee

read

Pete

Ii

high

sky

Oo

go

store

Uu

huge

cube

▶ Phonics

Write the correct word in each space.

| of   mother   brother   other   one |

1. My __brother__ and sister are younger than I am.

2. We had __one__ hour to write a paper.

3. I had a scoop __of__ ice cream.

4. Both my __mother__ and father work.

5. It is either one or the __other__.

UNIT 7   Keep Trying • **Lesson 5** *The Way of an Ant*

▶ Completing Sentences

Circle the correct word.
Write it in the space.

1. You only live __once__.

2. I __love__ my new puppy.

3. The store had __none__ left.

4. Can you __come__ over after school?

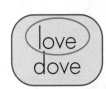

5. Would you like __some__ more?

Phonics   Write *alk*. Match each word with the correct picture.

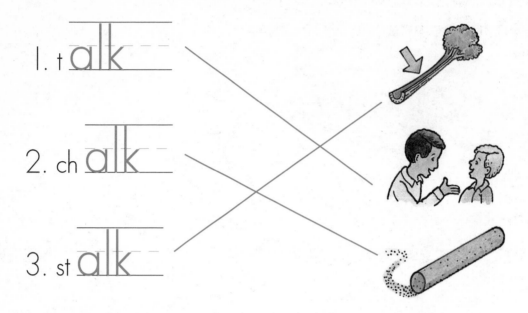

1. t alk

2. ch alk

3. st alk

Write *all* in each space. Then match it with the correct picture.

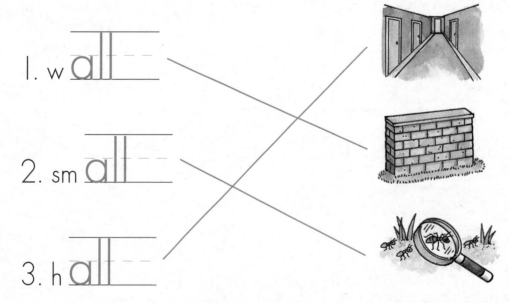

1. w all

2. sm all

3. h all

UNIT 7   **Keep Trying • Lesson 7** *The Hare and the Tortoise*

Completing Sentences

Circle the correct word. Write it in the space.

1. Jimmy and Pam play catch with a __ball__.
   bawl (ball)

2. May we use __chalk__ to color the picture?
   (chalk) calk

3. Patty hung a poster on her bedroom __wall__.
   (wall) walk

4. The __stalk__ of corn is five feet tall.
   stall (stalk)

5. Our classroom is down this __hall__.
   (hall) hawk

6. I need to __talk__ to my mother.
   (talk) tall

7. Matt and Jeff like to __walk__ to the park.
   wall (walk)

▶ **Phonics**   Write *oo* or *u* to complete each word.

ball<u>oo</u>n

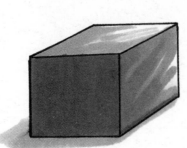

c<u>u</u>be

gl<u>u</u>e

m<u>u</u>sic

m<u>oo</u>n

st<u>oo</u>l

b<u>oo</u>t

r<u>u</u>ler

racc<u>oo</u>n

Completing Sentences

Circle the word that is spelled correctly.
Then write it in the space.

1. Mark swims in the __pool__.

   pule (pool)

2. The __mule__ would not pull the cart.

   (mule) moole

3. Beth tossed the basketball into the __hoop__.

   hupe (hoop)

4. We go to the lunchroom at __noon__.

   (noon) nune

5. Can you __use__ this box for toys?

   ooze (use)

6. We need to leave very __soon__.

   (soon) sune

Phonics

Write *au*.
Then write the whole word in the space.

1. au to   auto

2. c au se   cause

3. bec au se   because

Write *augh*.
Then write the whole word in the space.

1. t augh t   taught

2. c augh t   caught

3. d augh ter   daughter

Name _____ Date _____

 Completing Sentences

Circle the word that is spelled correctly.
Then write it in the space.

1. Mom _____taught_____ us how to make muffins.

   tot (taught)

2. Ted missed the show _____because_____ he was sick.

   (because) becaughse

3. Dad drove his new _____auto_____ to work.

   (auto) otto

4. It is Martha's _____fault_____ that we are late.

   falt (fault)

5. Pat _____caught_____ the puppy as it ran past him.

   cot (caught)

UNIT 8   Games • **Lesson 4** *Mary Mack*

▶ **Phonics**   Read the paragraph. Write the underlined words under the correct picture.

Genna the Gardener

<u>Genna</u> likes to work in the <u>garden</u> behind her <u>cottage</u>. She <u>grows</u> many things like <u>green</u> beans and <u>cabbage</u>. She has the <u>biggest</u> carrots in town. Genna likes to <u>give</u> her pals <u>Ginger</u>, <u>Gail</u>, and <u>Ginny</u> the things she grows in her garden.

Genna   Ginger

cottage   Ginny

cabbage

UNIT 8   Games • **Lesson 4** *Mary Mack*

garden

grows

green

biggest

give

Gail

▶ **Phonics**   Write the correct word in each space.

1. We watched the chipmunk __climb__ the tree.
   trim   climb

2. The bird sat on the tree __limb__ .
   limb   limp

3. Would you like a glass of __water__ ?
   winter   water

4. A __lamb__ has a soft coat.
   lamb   lamp

5. I took the dog for a __walk__ .
   work   walk

Reading and Writing

Write the sentence that goes with each picture.

The boy jumped into the water.

The boy ran from the wasp.

The boy ran from the wasp.

The lamb walked into the water.

The lion chased the lamb.

The lamb walked into the water.

The puppy played with the comb.

The puppy ate the crumbs.

The puppy ate the crumbs.

▶**Phonics**   Circle the words with the long *i* sound.
Write each word one time at the bottom.

The sun (shines) on the jungle. It makes patches of shade

and (light.) A (tiger) sits in the shadows. Her coat is gold (like)

the sun's (light.) It has (stripes) of black (like) the shade. The (tiger)

blends in with her jungle home.

shines   like

light   stripes

tiger

                              /ī/ *Spellings* • **Phonics Skills**

Write the words that rhyme.

| read   measure   bread   pleasure   spread |

treasure   measure   pleasure

head   read   bread

              spread

▶**Phonics** Circle the words with the long *u* sound.
Write each word one time at the bottom.

It was lunchtime. (Huey) was hungry. He looked at a

(menu) and ordered a (huge) sandwich. (Huey) had fun as he

waited for his lunch. He watched a lady (amuse) her (cute)

baby with a fuzzy toy. He saw a boy (argue) with his sister.

A few pups jumped up and down outside. At last (Huey) got

his sandwich.

Huey   amuse

menu   cute

huge   argue

UNIT 9 **Being Afraid • Lesson 4** *We're Going on a Bear Hunt*

Completing Sentences

Circle the word that completes each sentence.

1. The band plays nice (**music** must).

2. She had only a (dew **few**) dollars left.

3. The truck was (hug **huge**).

4. What a (**cute** cut) baby!

5. Please (us **use**) the front exit.

Phonics   Find the words that match the foot
picture or the goo picture.

Brad Cooks

It was almost (noon.) Brad wanted to (cook.) He (took) out a (cookbook.) He used a big (spoon) to make the batter (smooth.) Then he put his (cookies) in the oven. Brad used a (broom) to sweep up his mess. He (shook) his apron. When the (cookies) were done, he let them (cool.)

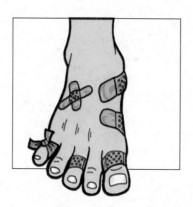

cook	cookies
took	shook
cookbook	

noon

spoon

smooth

broom

cool

UNIT 9 Being Afraid • **Lesson 10** *The Three Billy Goats Gruff*

▷ **Phonics**   Write the word that best completes each sentence.

| hair   picture   hear   shore   fire |

1. Did you <u>hear</u> the bell ring?

2. I will put more logs on the <u>fire</u>.

3. Dad went to get his <u>hair</u> cut.

4. Sara drew a <u>picture</u> of her house.

5. We walked along the sandy <u>shore</u>.

UNIT 9   **Being Afraid • Lesson 10** *The Three Billy Goats Gruff*

▶ **Reading and Writing**   Write the sentence that matches each picture.

The store sells teddy bears.

The store sells flowers.

The store sells teddy bears.

We looked at the pretty pictures.

We could hear the music.

We could hear the music.

Jane has long, red hair.

Mort poured the mixture.

Mort poured the mixture.

Phonics   Write the word that best completes each sentence.

| table   candle   supper   cattle   bottle |

1. Dad made meatloaf for _supper_.

2. We eat dinner at the kitchen _table_.

3. The baby drank milk from a _bottle_.

4. She always lights a _candle_ at night.

5. The _cattle_ graze on the farm.

▶ **Phonics** Write the words that rhyme.

judge	spice	rage	space	twice	budge
cage	race	age	mice	smudge	place

face ___race___ ___place___ ___space___

rice ___mice___ ___spice___ ___twice___

page ___age___ ___cage___ ___rage___

fudge ___judge___ ___budge___ ___smudge___

UNIT 10 Homes • **Lesson 7** *Home for a Bunny*

▶Phonics | Write *ey*. Write the whole word in the space. Match it with the correct picture.

1. turk __ey__   turkey

2. hon __ey__   honey

3. troll __ey__   trolley

4. k __ey__   key

5. monk __ey__   monkey

/ē/ *Spelled* ey • Phonics Skills

UNIT 10 Homes • **Lesson 7** *Home for a Bunny*

Completing Sentences

Circle and write the word that is spelled correctly.

1. Spilled glue made a _____ gooey _____ mess.

   (gooey) gooy

2. Ann slammed the  volleyball over the net.

   vollyball (volleyball)

3. The warm fire made the cabin very _____ homey _____.

   (homey) homy

4. They went on a long _____ journey _____ across the sea.

   (journey) journy

5. Mom put some _____ barley _____ in the vegetable soup.

   barly (barley)

▶ **Phonics**   Write *ion* or *tion* in each space to complete each sentence.

1. The movie was filled with ac tion .

2. The on ion had a strong odor.

3. Pay atten tion in class.

4. Ben won a mill ion dollars.

5. Don't be afraid to ask a ques tion .

6. We took a long vaca tion .

UNIT 10 **Homes • Lesson 8** *Is This a House for Hermit Crab?*

Write the words that rhyme.

| motion | station | potion |
| billion | vacation | trillion |

1. nation station vacation

2. lotion motion potion

3. million billion trillion